Webster's Contemporary
School & Office Dictionary